Publisher`s Note:
Please note that the German and English versions of the story were written to be as close as possible. However, in some cases they may differ in order to accomodate the nuances and fluidity of each language. Author, translator, and publisher made every effort to ensure accuracy. We therefore take no responsibility for inconsistency and minor errors.

Translated by the author
Illustrations by Supuni Suriyarachchi
Copy design and book layout by Emy Farella

ISBN: 978-3-947410-68-2
1. Edition

INGO BLUM

The FLYING TREE

DER FLIEGENDE BAUM

Illustrated by
Supuni Suriyarachchi

Once on a hill there stood a tree.

He felt **lonely** and **bored** and wanted **to break free**.

Auf einem Hügel stand einmal ein Baum.

Er fühlte sich **einsam** und **gelangweilt** und **wollte frei sein**.

"I wish I could fly up in the **sky** and see
the world from above.
From this place I want to flee!"

6

„Ich wünschte, ich könnte in den **Himmel** fliegen und die Welt von oben sehen. Von diesem Ort möchte ich fliehen."

"No animal rests at my solid trunk.

No **bear**, no **deer**, not even a **skunk**."

„Kein Tier ruht an meinem festen Stamm

Kein **Bär**, kein **Hirsch**, nicht einmal ein **Stinktier**."

The spring came, and a swallow sat down
on the tree.

"Can you give me shelter?" she asked.

"Sure, **it's all free!**"

Der Frühling kam, und eine Schwalbe setzte
sich auf den Baum.

„Kannst du mir Unterschlupf geben?" fragte sie.

„Sicher, **es ist alles umsonst**!"

"**This place is so boring**", said the tree.
"I would love to see some other places."

"**I can do magic**," the swallow said.
"I know a lot of other spaces."

„**Dieser Ort ist langweilig**", sagte der Baum.
„Ich würde gerne mal andere Orte sehen."

„**Ich kann zaubern**", sagte die Schwalbe.
„Ich kenne viele andere Orte."

Suddenly, the tree felt like he was pulled out of the ground.

Plötzlich fühlte sich der Baum, als ob er aus dem Boden gezogen würde.

Suddenly, the tree felt like he was pulled out
of the ground.

All with his roots, with a cracking sound.
He was lifted up in the sky and heard the swallow cry,
"Use your **branches** to **move** and **fly!**"

Mit all seinen **Wurzeln**, mit einem
knackenden Geräusch.

Er wurde in den Himmel emporgehoben und hörte
die Schwalbe rufen: „Benutze deine **Äste**, um dich
zu **bewegen** und zu **fliegen**!"

The other trees stood in wonder, whispering
"Come back soon!"

The tree was very fast, hovering like a
wonderful balloon.

Die anderen Bäume standen staunend da und
flüsterten: **„Komm bald wieder!"**

Der Baum war schnell, schwebte wie ein
wunderbarer Ballon.

They flew over lakes, and forests,
and fields and over a cloud.

The tree cried "**yoo-hoo**", very loud.

Sie flogen über Seen und Wälder und Felder
und über eine Wolke.

Der Baum rief sehr laut „**Juhu**!"

Soon they came **into a fog**
and could not see.

The tree was exhausted,
but enjoyed **to be free**.

Bald kamen sie **in einen Nebel**
und konnten nichts mehr sehen.

Der Baum war erschöpft,
aber froh, **frei zu sein**.

"Do you like what you see,"
the swallow asked.

They looked back to a hill they just passed.

The tree nodded happily, but needed a rest.

He wished he could **build something**
like a swallow's nest.

„Gefällt dir, was du siehst?", fragte die **Schwalbe**.

Sie blickten zurück zu einem Hügel, an dem sie gerade
vorbeigekommen waren.

Der Baum nickte freudig, brauchte aber eine Pause.

Er wünschte sich, er könnte auch so **etwas wie
ein Schwalbennest bauen.**

When they landed on a mountain,
it was much **too cold**.

The tree did not like that.
The place was odd and old.

Als sie auf einem Berg landeten,
war es viel **zu kalt**.

Das gefiel dem Baum nicht.
Der Ort war **seltsam** und **alt**.

They carried on and came to a **big city**.
They saw some trees that didn't look very happy.

Sie flogen weiter und kamen in eine **große Stadt**.

Sie sahen einige Bäume, die nicht sehr glücklich aussahen.

The trees said "Dogs pee at us.
That's not nice!

We are city trees, so we have
to pay the price."

Die Bäume sagten: „Die Hunde pinkeln uns an.
Das ist nicht schön!

Wir sind Stadtbäume, also müssen wir den
Preis dafür zahlen."

"I want to see more," the tree
whooped with joy.

And made some somersaults in the air,
like a **little boy**.

„Ich will noch mehr sehen", **jubelte**
der Baum vor Freude.

Und er machte einige Purzelbäume in
der Luft, wie ein **kleiner Junge**.

They came to a desert
which was very hot.

Sie kamen in eine Wüste,
die sehr heiß war.

The swallow said "**This is a
desert, a very dry spot!**"

"Deserts are always dry,"
a palm tree said with a smile.

The tree quickly said,
"**Let's fly another mile!**"

Die Schwalbe sagte: „**Das ist eine Wüste,
ein sehr trockener Ort**!"

„Wüsten sind immer trocken",
sagte eine Palme mit einem Lächeln.

Der Baum sagte schnell:
„**Lass uns noch eine Meile
weiterfliegen!**"

In a **forest** they heard a loud, roaring noise.

In einem **Wald** hörten sie ein lautes, dröhnendes Geräusch.

They saw some loggers, with chainsaws,
one was shouting in an **angry voice**.

"They want to cut the trees!"
the swallow cried.

Again they flew up into the wide.

42

Sie sahen einige Holzfäller mit Kettensägen,
einer schrie mit **wütender Stimme**.

„Sie wollen die Bäume fällen!"
rief die Schwalbe.

Wieder flogen sie hinauf in die Ferne.

Early next morning they saw a hill not far away.

The sun was shining. It was a bright, **sunny day**.

Am nächsten Morgen sahen sie nicht weit entfernt einen Hügel. Die Sonne schien. Es war ein heller, **sonniger Tag**.

"This is my hill," the tree cried happily,
"this is my hood!"

And then he saw the big hole where he
once stood.

„**Das ist mein Hügel**", rief der Baum fröhlich,
„das ist meine Heimat!"

Und dann sah er das große Loch, in dem er
einst gestanden hatte.

Slowly he moved his **roots** to the hole, adjusting with care.

Langsam bewegte er seine **Wurzeln** in das Loch und passte sie vorsichtig an.

"**You are back!**" the other trees cried.
"How is the world out there?"

And the tree told them about his

adventures, closing with the **words**,

„**Du bist zurück**!", riefen die anderen Bäume.
„Wie sieht die Welt da draußen aus?"

Und der Baum erzählte ihnen von seinen

Abenteuern und schloss mit den **Worten**:

"There is no place like home!
I don't want to be like the birds."

„Es gibt keinen Ort wie Zuhause!
Ich will nicht wie die Vögel sein."

The little swallow nodded and smiled.
She has always known.

You leave a **big** hole when
you are leaving home.

Die kleine Schwalbe nickte und lächelte.
Sie hat es immer gewusst.

Man hinterlässt ein **großes** Loch,
wenn man seine Heimat verläßt.

More Bilingual Books

ISBN 979-8672025681

ISBN 979-8682547906

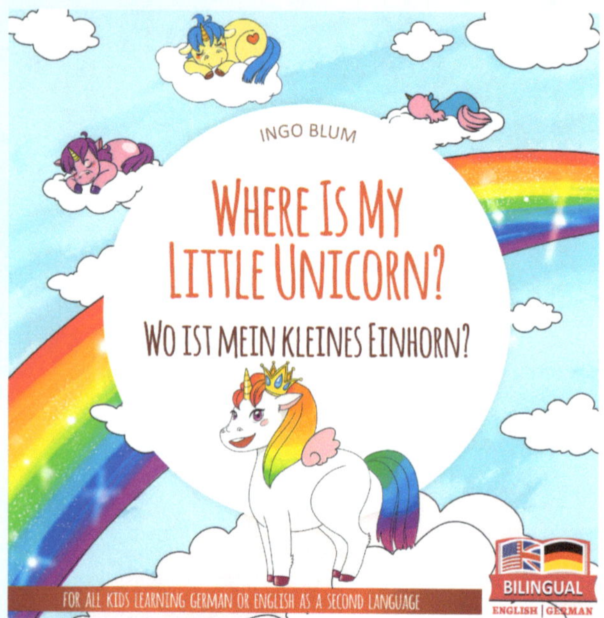

ISBN 979-8460931347

ISBN 978-1983093975